Non-Fiction Titles by Janvier T. Chando

HEGEMON IN THE MAKING: THE BIRTH AND GROWTH…
FALLEN HEROES: African Leaders Whose Assassinations…
ICONS AND VILLAINS: Recent Political Assassinations…
UKRAINE: The Tug-of-War Between Russia and the West
CAMEROON: The Haunted Heart of Africa

Fiction Titles by Janvier Chando

The Usurper: and Other Stories
Triple Agent, Double Cross
Disciples of Fortune
The Union Moujik
Flash of the Sun
Good Fortune Calls
Master of Good Fortune
Good Fortune's Children
The Girl on the Trail
Me Before Them
The Grandmothers and Perfect Love
The Fire and Ice Legend
The Sweetest Madness
The Hunger Fire
The Shades of Fire
Father and Sons
Fateful Ties
The Verdict of Hades
His Majesty's Trial
Ngoko's Folly
The Usurper
The Dowry
I am Hated
The Oaf

Upcoming Titles by Janvier Chando

The Home Drifters
The Mortal Friends
The White Hawk
The Norilsk Bears

BROKEN ESSENCE:
India, its Gandhi Heroes, their Assassinations and their Legacies

Janvier T. Chando

TISI BOOKS

NEW YORK, RALEIGH, LONDON, AMSTERDAM

BROKEN ESSENCE:

India, its Gandhi Heroes, their
Assassinations and their Legacies
Copyright © 2018 by Janvier T. Chando

ISBN-13: 978-1-9809-5023-3
ISBN-10: 1-9809-5023-7

PUBLISHED BY TISI BOOKS
www.tisibooks.com

NEW YORK, RALEIGH, LONDON, AMSTERDAM

Printed in The United States of America

EPIGRAPH

"Destiny is something we can only contemplate; but fate, we can influence."

—CHRISTOPHER NKWAYEP-CHANDO

ACKNOWLEDGEMENT

My deepest, warmest and everlasting thanks to Dr. Samuel F. Tchwenko and Christopher N. Chando for their contributions to the ideal of social solidarity and the enhancement of humanity.

DEDICATION

The book is dedicated to all iconic and legendary leaders whose purposes were to serve humanity and advance the wellbeing of mankind, especially those who were cut short in their historic missions by the evil forces of this world.

BROKEN ESSENCE:
India, its Gandhi Heroes, their Assassinations and their Legacies

Contents

MAPS

India on a Map of the World

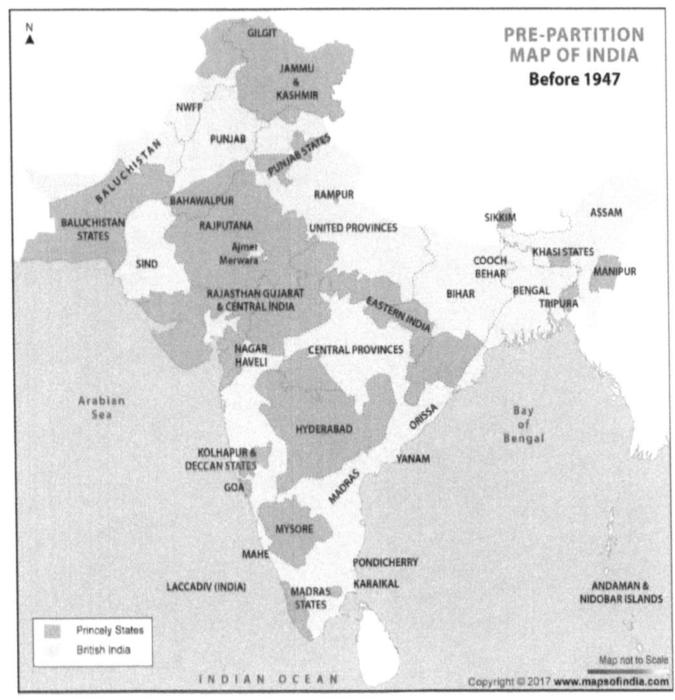

States from Partitioned India

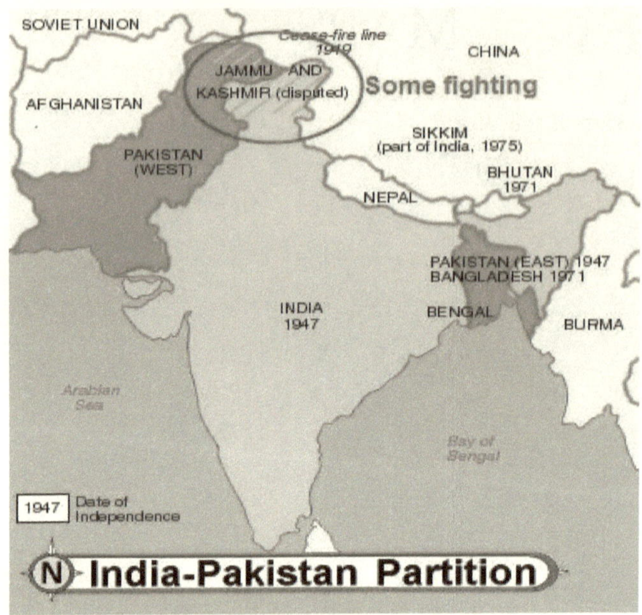

New Map of the Indian Subcontinent after 1971

INTRODUCTION

In my search for the answer to why certain geopolitical flashpoints exist in the world, in my pry to know the reason (s) why some countries and the world in general experienced sudden and dramatic changes that led to war, instability or a reorientation of their domestic and foreign policies that not only affected these countries but also influence certain regions or the whole world, I explored political assassinations over the past dozens of decades that changed our world. By our world, I mean our communities, countries, regions and humanity as a whole.

In treating the different assassinations that took place over the years, I used an approach characterized by political sociology, where I succinctly analyzed the historical and social factors that not only led to the assassinations, but that also arose from the killing of these historical figures. And from these factors, we are presented with an idea or pictures of how the society affected has evolved since the traumatic event (s).

From the backlashes that followed the assassination of

historic, legendary or iconic figures, we can learn something useful and come up with scenarios or what to expect as calamities if particular leaders are assassinated, and so act accordingly in preventing their assassinations.

CHAPTER ONE

Mohandas "Mahatma" Gandhi

Mahatma Gandhi Quotes

"Be the change that you wish to see in the world."

"Where there is love, there is life."

"What difference does it make to the dead, the orphans and the homeless, whether the mad destruction is wrought under the name of totalitarianism or in the holy name of liberty or democracy?"

"I like your Christ, I do not like your Christians. Your Christians are so unlike your Christ."

"Live as if you were to die tomorrow. Learn as if you were to live forever."

"The best way to find yourself is to lose yourself in the service of others."

"Prayer is the key of the morning and the bolt of the evening."

"A man who was completely innocent, offered himself as a sacrifice for the good of others, including his enemies, and became the ransom of the world. It was a perfect act."

"First they ignore you, then they laugh at you, then they fight you, then you win."

"Happiness is when what you think, what you say, and what you do are in harmony."

"You must not lose faith in humanity. Humanity is an ocean; if a few drops of the ocean are dirty, the ocean does not become dirty."

"An eye for an eye will only make the whole world blind."

"In a gentle way, you can shake the world."

"When I despair, I remember that all through history the way of truth and love have always won. There have been tyrants and murderers, and for a time, they can seem invincible, but in the end, they always fall. Think of it--always."

"God has no religion."

"The weak can never forgive. Forgiveness is the attribute of the strong."

"Action expresses priorities."

"Prayer is not asking. It is a longing of the soul. It is daily admission of one's weakness. It is better in prayer to have a heart without words than words without a heart."

"Strength does not come from physical capacity. It comes from an indomitable will."

"A man is but the product of his thoughts; what he thinks, he becomes."

"Earth provides enough to satisfy every man's needs, but not every man's greed."

"Freedom is not worth having if it does not include the freedom to make mistakes."

"Hate the sin, love the sinner."

"Whatever you do will be insignificant, but it is very important that you do it."

"Earth provides enough to satisfy every man's needs, but not every man's greed."

India on the Map of the World

Administrative Map of India

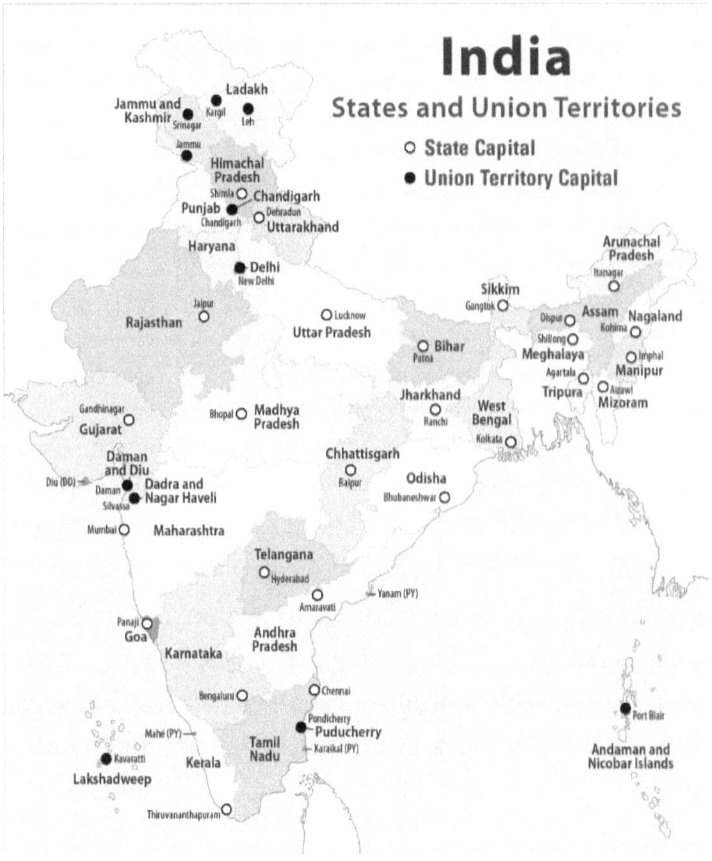

Map of India before the Partition

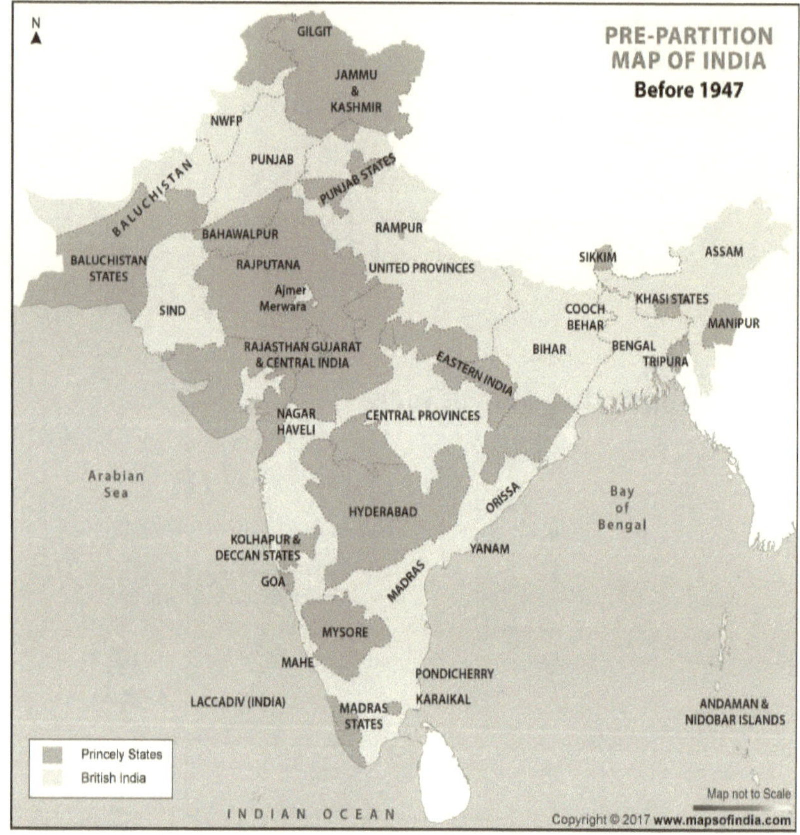

Mohandas Karamchand Gandhi, popularly known as Mahatma" Gandhi, led the nationalist movement against British rule in the Indian subcontinent, and is considered in many circles as the father of modern-day India, Bangladesh, and Pakistan. He is highly esteemed internationally for his doctrine of nonviolent protest to achieve political and social progress. However, one of the greatest disappointments of Gandhi's life was the fact that the Indian freedom (freedom for the entire subcontinent) he suffered so much for was realized without Indian unity, as two separate countries—Indian and Pakistan (West Pakistan and East Pakistan or what became Bangladesh on 26 March 1971) emerged from the non-violent liberation struggle he led against British colonial rule—Pakistan for Muslims and India for Hindus. His effort to mitigate the growing sectarian divide was cut short by Nathuram Godse, a young Hindu fanatic, who shot him on January 30, 1948, in Delhi, while he was on his way to his evening prayer.

How did the little man who made three continents home emerge as such an international icon?

Born on 2 October 1869 as the son and youngest child of Karamchand Uttamchand Gandhi (1822–1885), who served as the diwan (chief minister) of Porbandar state in India, and his fourth wife, Putlibai, the young Gandhi did not achieve academic excellence until after he left India for London to study law in 1888. He returned to India shortly after he got called to the bar in June 1891, and set about establishing a law practice in Bombay. However, he was unsuccessful in his efforts. Not until an Indian firm offered him a one-year contract to work for them in the Colony of Natal, South Africa, which was also a part of the British Empire, did a major chapter of his life begin. Even so, he left for South Africa with no clear-cut plans.

The racism, prejudice, and injustice against people of color in South Africa, and more so the discrimination the Indians there were subjected to, made Gandhi start questioning his place in the South African society. That period proved to be a turning point in his life as it shaped his social activism and opened his eyes to social injustice. But it wasn't until in 1906, after the Transvaal government promulgated a new Act compelling the colony's Indian and Chinese populations to register, and these communities decided to protest that Gandhi the activist was born.

It was during the protest that Gandhi adopted his nascent and evolving methodology of Satyagraha (devotion to the truth) or nonviolent protest, for the first time. He urged Indians to defy the new law and be prepared to suffer the punishments for their stance. The adoption of this plan by the Indian Community would mean that thousands of Indians were jailed, flogged, or shot for their nonviolent resistance during the ensuing seven-year struggle. That period of struggle saw Gandhi's ideas take shape and the concept of Satyagraha mature. Thereafter, he pursued his political activism in the context of his South African law practice.

Gandhi returned to India in 1915 as a proficient public speaker and as someone adept at fund-raising, negotiations, media relations, and self-promotion. Right after his return, he became a formidable asset for the Indian Congress Party. As a leading Indian nationalist, theorist and organizer, he transformed the Indian Congress party into a wholly Indian political movement and escalated the party's objectives to the point where it declared the independence of India on 26 January 1930, a move the British colonial administration did not recognize, but one that compelled it to start consulting the Congress party in the administration of the subcontinent and in the charting of its future relations. His opposition to the fact that the British colonial administration dragged India into World War Two without contacting and consulting the Indian people about it, brought him and the Congress party into loggerheads with the British. Also, his 1942 demand for immediate independence for India prompted the British to imprison him and tens of thousands of leaders of the Congress Party.

The South Asian Language Groups

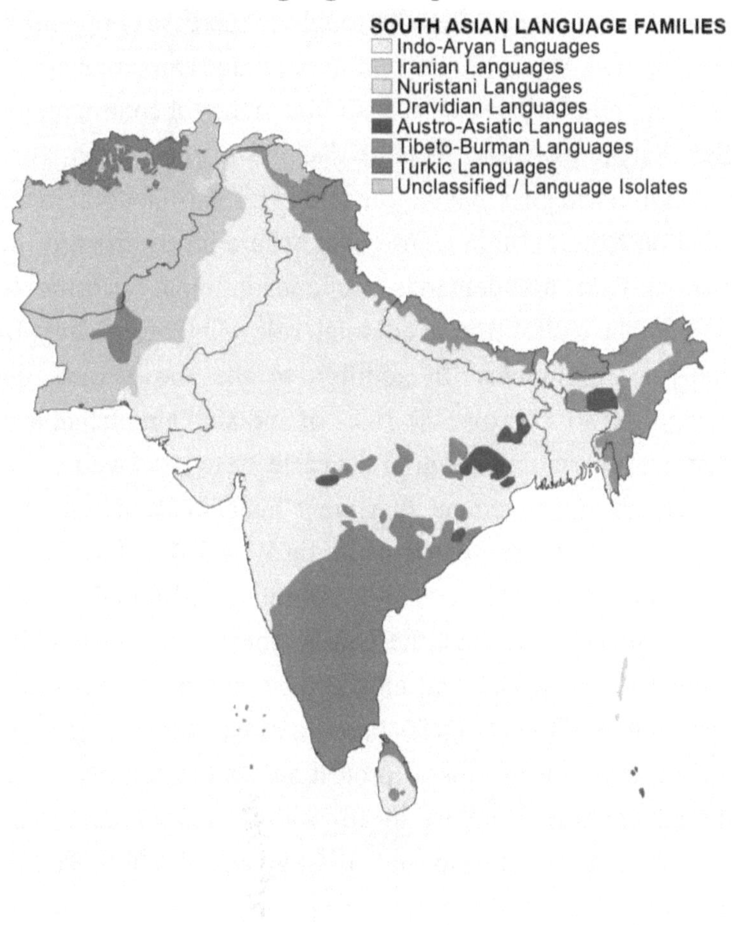

The fact that more than 2. 5 million Indians volunteered and fought with the British Army against Germany and its allies during the war showed that this was perhaps the only pre-independence campaign that Gandhi did not get right. But before that, he was on spot on such previous campaigns as the recruitment of Indians to fight for the British in World War One, his support of the peasants against the British landlords and the local administrations in 1918, the 1919 Khilafat movement where he sought to increase cooperation with India's Muslims, the non-cooperation campaign aimed at forcing the collapse of British rule in the subcontinent, the Salt Satyagraha (Salt March) that led to the March 1931 Gandhi–Irwin Pact that culminated in his participation in the London Round Table Conference where he confronted the British with his demands for constitutional reforms to prepare the end of British colonial rule and the beginning of self-rule by Indians. In addition to the above were his campaigns to improve the lives of India's "Untouchables" that put him in opposition to the caste system, as well as his "Quit India" Movement that went hand in hand with his opposition to India's participation in World War Two.

However, it was Gandhi's Bombay (Mumbai) "Quit India" speech that gave the British colonial authorities the pretext to arrest him and all the members of the Working Committee of the Congress Party, a move that ignited riots, arsons, and other forms of protest across the country, even though he was steadfast in advocating non-violence. His release came about on 6 May 1944 against the backdrop of his failing health, the deaths of his wife of sixty years and his long-time secretary, as well as against an altered political landscape where the once marginal Muslim League political party that had cooperated with Britain during the war was now posing as a formidable rival to the Indian Congress party.

Proportion of Muslims in British India in 1941

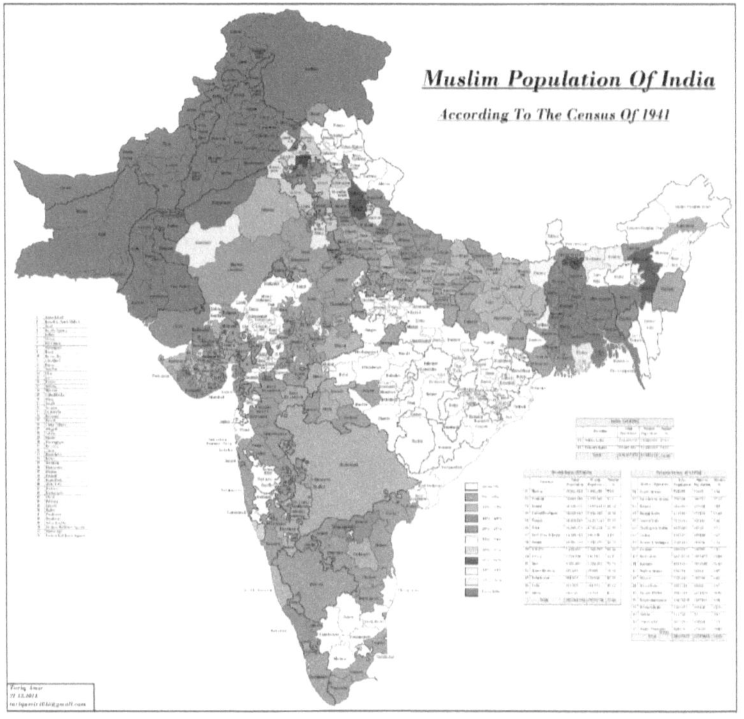

Gandhi, who had always supported a religiously diverse India, was taken aback by the Muslim League's demands for a separate Muslim state of Pakistan. Helpless, he watched Britain partition the land along religious lines, giving India and Pakistan independence on terms that failed to meet Gandhi's expectations.

Pundits hold that Muslim separatism only received a great boost while Gandhi and his colleagues of the Congress Party were in jail. In fact, while the final constitutional arrangements were being negotiated in 1946–1947, communal riots between Hindus and Muslims rocked the subcontinent, thereby undermining Gandhi's appeals to reason and justice, tolerance, and trust. With the partition of the subcontinent accepted by both the Hindu and Muslim political elites against his noble advice, he made it his mission to heal the scars of the communal conflict. That saw him touring riot-torn areas in Bengal and Bihar; that saw him rebuking the bigots on both sides of the religious divide; and that led him to the victims as he consoled them and led efforts to rehabilitate the refugees.

But the fallout of the partition, which directly or indirectly led to the deaths of about 2 million people, had already created an atmosphere of hatred and suspicion that even the peaceful Gandhi could not reverse. As a matter of fact, both Hindu and Muslim radicals blamed him. But he was relentless and even took to fasting to make his point. Sometimes his fasting failed to mitigate the situation, but other times it helped to convince both communities to make an effort to get along. A case in point where Gandhi's fasting eased the tension between the Hindu and Muslim communities was in September 1947 when it stopped rioting in Calcutta, and in January 1948 when it led to a communal truce in Delhi.

Mahatma Gandhi did not harbor any plan to stop his fasting campaign as he left his current residence on 30 January 1948 and made his way to prayer, only to be stopped by a young Hindu fanatic Nathuram Godse who shot him three times at point-blank range. It happened as he was walking in the private garden of the house of the Biria family, escorted by four women and members of the household. He died on the spot. Godse was immediately apprehended, and he and his co-conspirator were tried and executed on November 15, 1949.

Mahatma Gandhi's death was mourned nationwide, with over two million people participating in the five-mile-long funeral procession from the house where he was assassinated to Raj Ghat on the banks of the Yamuna river where he was cremated. His ashes, which were supposed to be spread on a river, were instead placed in several urns that were eventually spread in several rivers across India and even abroad in such faraway places as the source of the River Nile near the Ugandan settlement of Jinga, in Africa. Curiously enough, an urn with his ashes graces the palace of the Aga Khan, where he was imprisoned from 1942 to 1944, while another urn is regarded as sacred in the Self-Realization Fellowship Lake Shrine in Los Angeles, California, USA.

Many reasons or excuses have been given as to why Nathuram Godse took away the life of such a pacifist. But the most widely held explanation put forward by some people who spoke with the assassin is that he believed Mahatma Gandhi treated Muslims with more respect than Hindus, which is curious indeed. All the same, the fact that Nathuram Godse was a Hindu, like Gandhi himself, was used effectively by the new government in India to abate the Hindu-Muslim acrimony that was going on in the new country.

The assassination of Mahatma Gandhi turned out to be useful in the sense that it created the grounds for a Muslim-Hindu reconciliation and religious tolerance in India that Pakistan never achieved because most Indians heeded the call to honor Mahatma Gandhi's memory and more so his ideals of religious tolerance, peace, harmony and love of humanity among other things. As a matter of fact, he is widely described in India as the "Father of the Nation", and his birthday on October 02 is a national holiday in India called Gandhi Jayanti.

India Before and after Partition

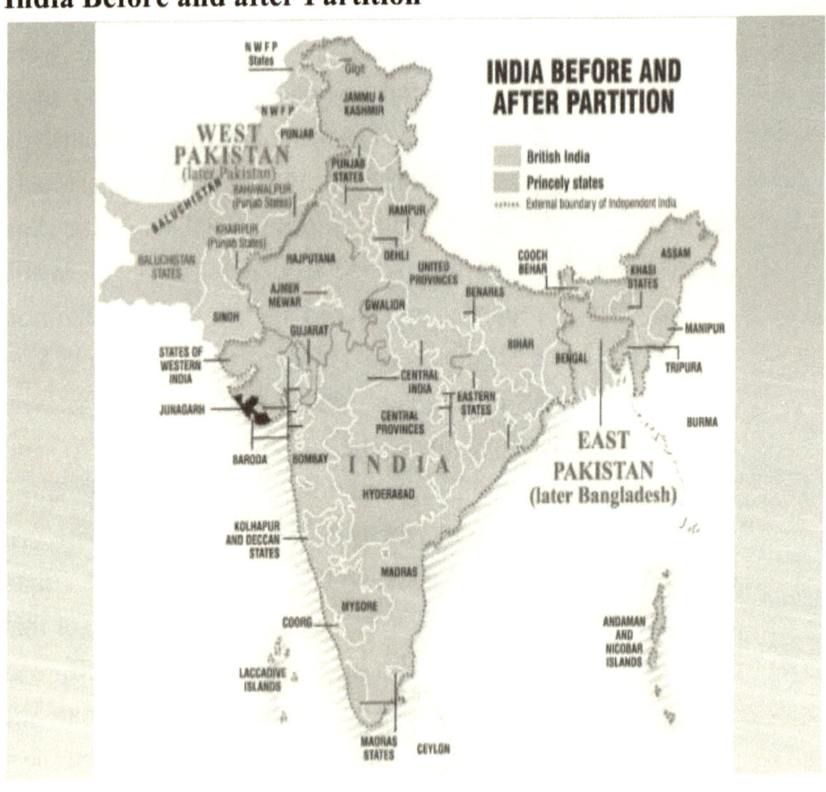

Some analysts view Mahatma Gandhi as a paragon of ethical living and pacifism, while others think he was a very complex and evolving character full of inner contradictions and influenced by his culture and the circumstances he found himself in. Even so, his principles, beliefs, and practices continue to inspire thinkers, altruists, and advocates of social solidarity today, especially those trying to right the wrongs of their societies, governments, and countries.

While many people and cultures influenced him, many pundits consider his biggest source of foreign influence to have come from the iconic Russian writer Leo oy whose 1894 non-fiction book "The Kingdom of God Is Within You" and 1908 letter written to the anti-British Bengali Indian revolutionary and internationalist scholar Tarak Nath Das, which was entitled "A Letter to a Hindu", left indelible impressions on Mahatma Gandhi and fundamentally influenced his method of passive resistance.

The word Mahatma became affixed to Gandhi's name only after his death, in recognition of his immense contribution to the destiny of the people of the Indian subcontinent and to humanity as a whole. It came from the Sanskrit words *maha* (meaning Great) and *atma* (meaning Soul).

Today, more than 50, 000 pages of Gandhi's works are published; innumerable streets, roads, and localities in India are named after him; and he is known all over the world. It is a widely held view that he greatly influenced important leaders and political movements such as Martin Luther King Jr., James Lawson, James Bevel, Nelson Mandela, and Aung San Suu Kyi.

Gandhi was a Time magazine "Man of the Year" award winner in 1930, and he was the runner-up to Albert Einstein as "Person of the Century", which is a compilation of the 20th century's 100 most influential people, published by Time magazine in 1999 and 2007.

The United Nations General Assembly declared Gandhi's October 02 birthday as "The International Day of Nonviolence." In fact, the life story and ideals of Mahatma Gandhi are widely available in literature, film, and theatre in India and abroad. Numerous biographies have been written about his life, making him one of the most written about, yet enigmatic figures of our times to have graced the world's political landscape.

Majority Religions in Pakistan, India, Nepal, Bhutan and Bangladesh

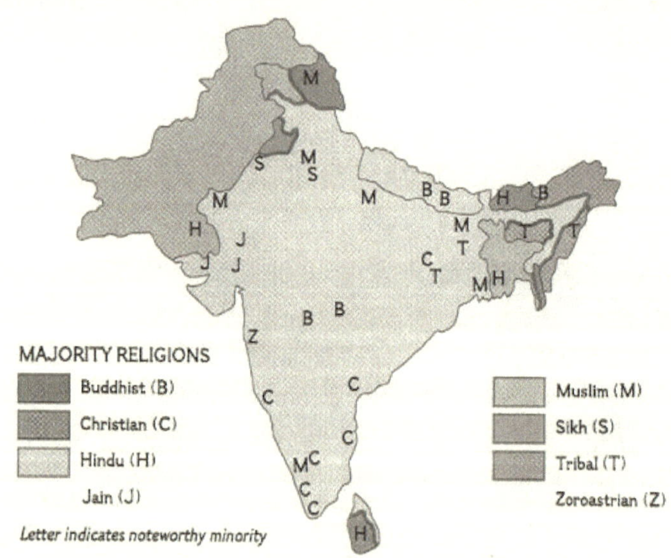

States from Partitioned India

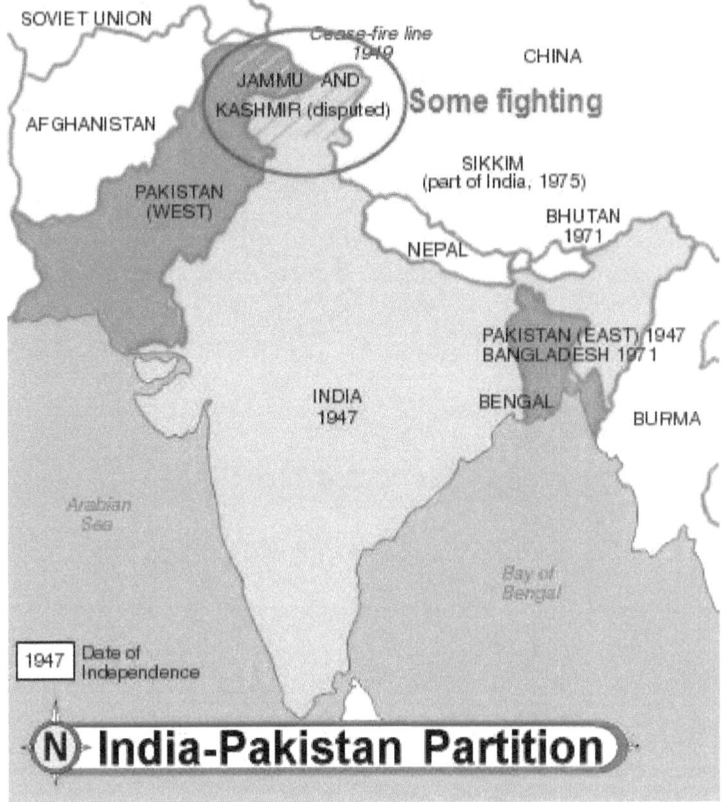

CHAPTER TWO

Indira Gandhi

Indira Gandhi Quotes

"You cannot shake hands with a clenched fist."

"There are two kinds of people, those who do the work and those who take the credit. Try to be in the first group; there is less competition there."

"You must learn to be still in the midst of activity and to be vibrantly alive in repose."

"Forgiveness is a virtue of the brave."

"The power to question is the basis of all human progress."

"People tend to forget their duties but remember their rights."

"A nation's strength ultimately consists in what it can do on its own, and not in what it can borrow from others."

"Education is a liberating force, and in our age it is also a democratizing force, cutting across the barriers of caste and class, smoothing out inequalities imposed by birth and other circumstances."

"Whenever you take a step forward, you are bound to disturb something."

"Martyrdom does not end something, it is only a beginning."

"The meek may one day inherit the earth, but not the headlines."

"The immediate is often the enemy of the ultimate."

"My father was a statesman, I am a political woman. My father was a saint. I am not."

"There exists no politician in India daring enough to attempt to explain to the masses that cows can be eaten."

"Life is a continuous process of adjustment."

"Without courage, you cannot practice any other virtue. You have to have courage - courage of different kinds: first, intellectual courage, to sort out different values and make up your mind about which is the one which is right for you to follow. You have to have moral courage to stick up to that - no matter what comes in your way, no matter what the obstacle and the opposition is."

"There is not love where there is no will."

"One must beware of ministers who can do nothing without money, and those who want to do everything with money."

"If I die a violent death, as some fear and a few are plotting, I know that the violence will be in the thought and the action of the assassins, not in my dying."

"Opportunities are not offered. They must be wrested and worked for. And this calls for perseverance... and courage."

India on the Map of the World

Administrative Map of India

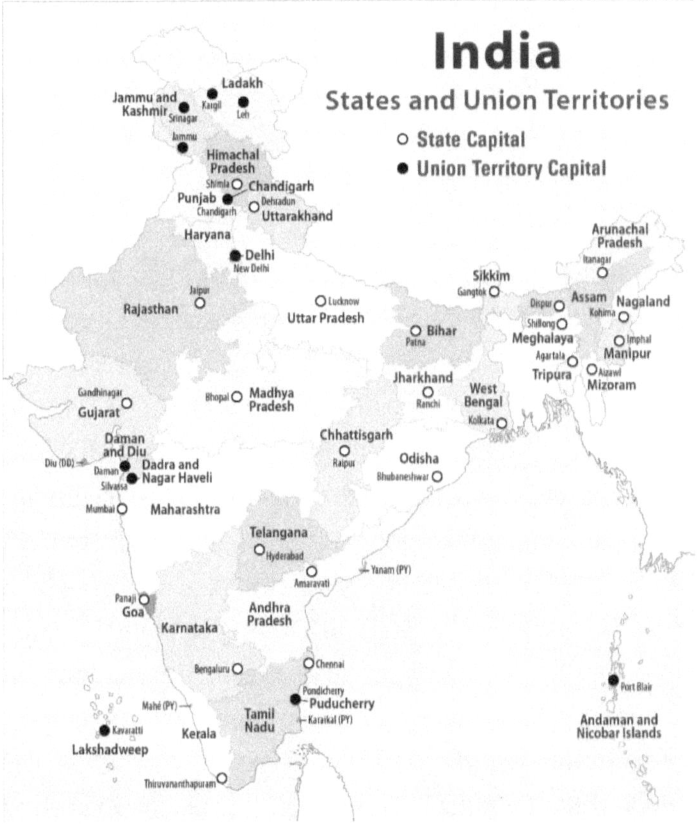

Indira Gandhi, the only child of Jawaharlal Nehru, the first prime minister of independent India, served as prime minister of India from 1966–77, spent three years in the opposition, and was serving a fourth term in office from 1980 when her life and rule was cut short by the bullets of an assassin.

Indira Gandhi did not succeed her father Nehru after he died in 1964 as many had speculated. In fact, Nehru was succeeded by La Bahadur Shastri, who served as India's prime minister until he too died suddenly in January 1966. Indira Gandhi, who had been in the cabinet or had been serving as a member of the Congress Party since 1955, succeeded La Bahadur Shastri as the new leader of the ruling party—and by default the new prime minister of India following a compromise between the right and left wings of the Congress Party.

The most remarkable highlight of Indira Gandhi's first three terms in office was the defeat of Pakistan in December 1971 when Indian forces had a decisive victory over Pakistan in what historians call the liberation war that led to the formation of an independent Bangladesh from what was East Pakistan. Even so, the victory against Pakistan did not pay political dividends for long as the Congress government was confronted with numerous problems, some of which were as a result of the high inflation brought about by wartime expenses, a drought that crippled aggriculture in many parts of the country, and more importantly, the 1973 oil crisis following the 1973 Arab-Israel war when the members of the Organization of Arab Petroleum Exporting

Countries (OPEC) proclaimed an oil embargo that drove up the price for oil, thereby crippling non-oil producing countries like India. Even so, the Congress Party would stay in power in India until 1977 largely through the declaration of a state of emergency throughout India, the imprisoning of political opponents, the use of emergency powers, and the passing of laws limiting personal freedoms. Historians hold that Indira Gandhi's younger son Sanjay played an outsized role in influencing her rule during the mid-1970s.

Extending the state of emergency twice did not help Indira Gandhi. A split in the Congress party saw veteran Indira Gandhi supporters like Jajuan Ram, Hematic Nandan Bhuna, and Nandini Sampath parting ways with her and forming a new political entity called CFD (Congress for Democracy), thereby making victory possible for the Janata Alliance of Opposition parties—an alliance made up of the right-wing Hindu leaning Bhartiya Jana Sangh, the Socialist parties, Congress (O), and Bhartiya Kranti Dal Party under Charon Singh that was representing the interests of northern peasants and farmers—to win the 1977 elections and come to power under the leadership of Morarji Desai. However, the Congress Party with Gandhi at its helm would regroup and return to power following the January 1980 elections.

Indira Gandhi was still savoring her return to power when on 23 June 1980, her close confidante in the person of her son Sanjay Gandhi died in an air crash while performing an aerobatic maneuver. When the grieving prime minister reluctantly brought in her pilot son, Rajiv, into politics, it was an indication of her lack of trust in others outside of her family.

Language Families or Groups in India, Pakistan, Bangladesh, Nepal and Bhutan

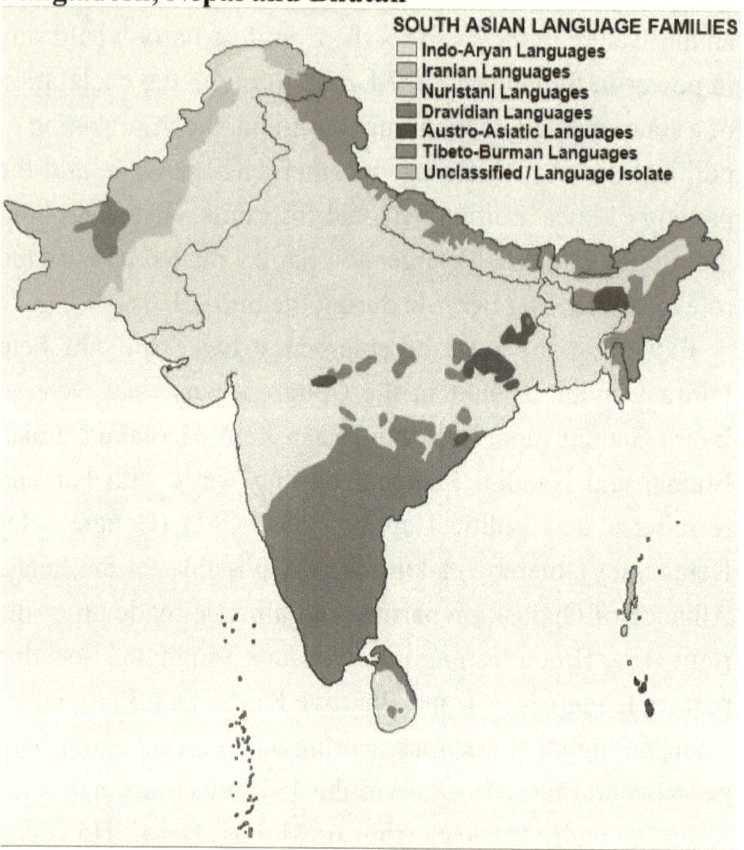

Indira Gandhi's fourth term in office was tumultuous as the political integrity of India was threatened from multiple fronts. Several states in the country sought greater autonomy or independence from the central government in Delhi. But nowhere was this surge more virulent than in Punjab where Jarnail Singh Bhindranwale, the leader of the Sikh organization Damdami Taksal, and a notable supporter of the 1973 Anandpur Resolution that among other things demanded the return of Chandigarh (a city and a union territory that serves as the capital of both neighboring states of Haryana and Punjab, and which is governed directly by the Union Government in Delhi) to Punjab, a demand Indira Gandhi viewed as a step towards secession by Punjab.

Bhindranwale was also championing Sikh separatists in the state of Punjab who were using violence to assert their demands for an autonomous state to the point where they turned the Sikhs' holiest shrine, the Harmandir Sahib (Golden Temple) at Amritsar into a fort that they used to commit murders.

Languages of India

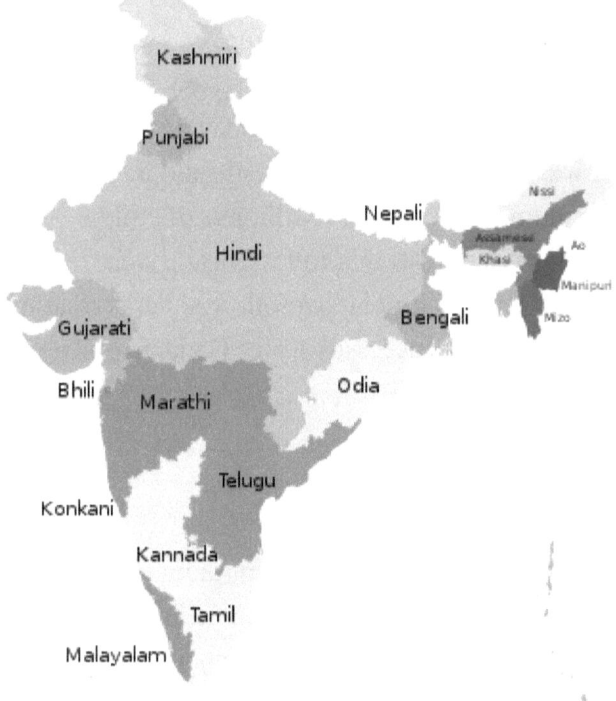

Indira Gandhi's rule would have lasted longer had her government succeeded in administering justice over those that were accused in negotiations that among other things called for the militants to leave the temple. But the negotiations failed, prompting her in June 1984 to order the Indian Army to enter the Golden Temple and remove Bhindranwale and his supporters from the complex. The storming of the temple resulted in the deaths of a large number of Sikh fighters and innocent pilgrims, with estimates ranging from several hundred to several thousand. So, when on October 31, 1984, two of her own Sikh bodyguards killed her by firing a fusillade of bullets in revenge for the attack on the Golden Temple, some pundits were quick to say that they saw it coming.

Indira Gandhi's corpse was cremated on 3 November near Raj Ghat, in a site that is known today as Shakti Sthal. Her funeral was watched live on domestic and international stations, including the BBC. Millions of Sikhs were displaced in the civil unrests that followed and close to three thousand died in anti-Sikh riots that followed her cremation, prompting her son and successor Rajiv Gandhi to state on TV that:

"When a big tree falls, the earth shakes."

Indira Gandhi is not only remembered in India for defeating Pakistan and making East Pakistan become an independent country called Bangladesh, but she is also cherished for making India a military power with atomic weapons, following the country's first successful nuclear bomb test on 18 May 1974. Prominent structures in the country named after her include the world's largest university called The Indira Gandhi National Open University and the Indira Gandhi International Airport, all in Delhi. Awards, Prizes, a low-cost housing program, and geographic points in India are also named after her. In 2011, Bangladesh posthumously conferred on Indira Gandhi the country's highest civilian award, which is called "The Bangladesh Freedom Honor (Bangladesh Swadhinata Sammanona)".

Map of Religious Minorities in India

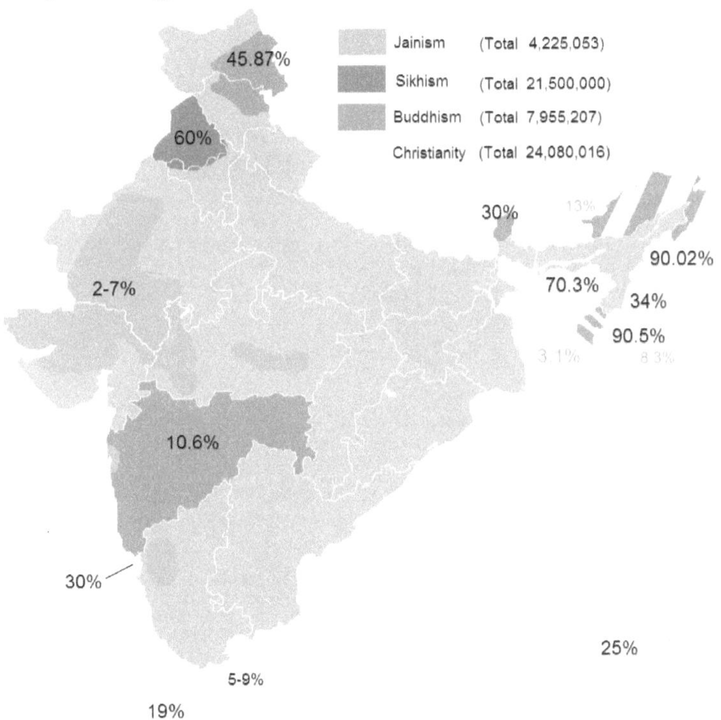

The Muslim Population of India

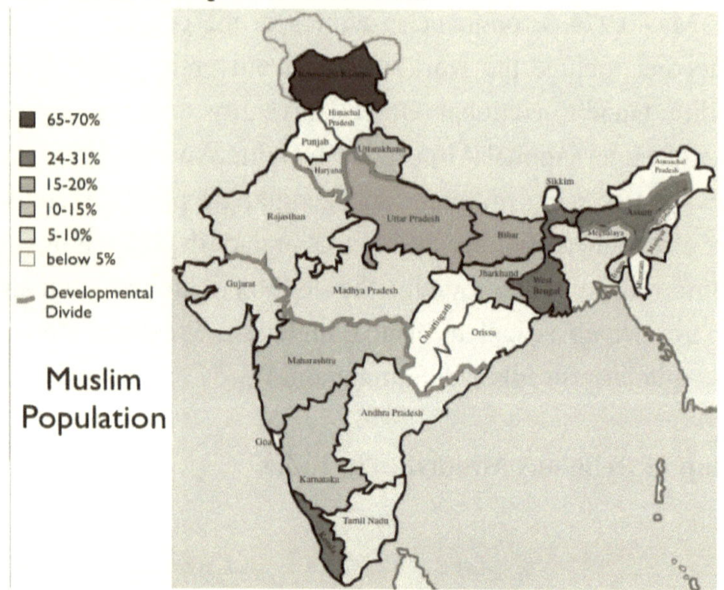

Majority Religions in Pakistan, India, Nepal, Bhutan and Bangladesh

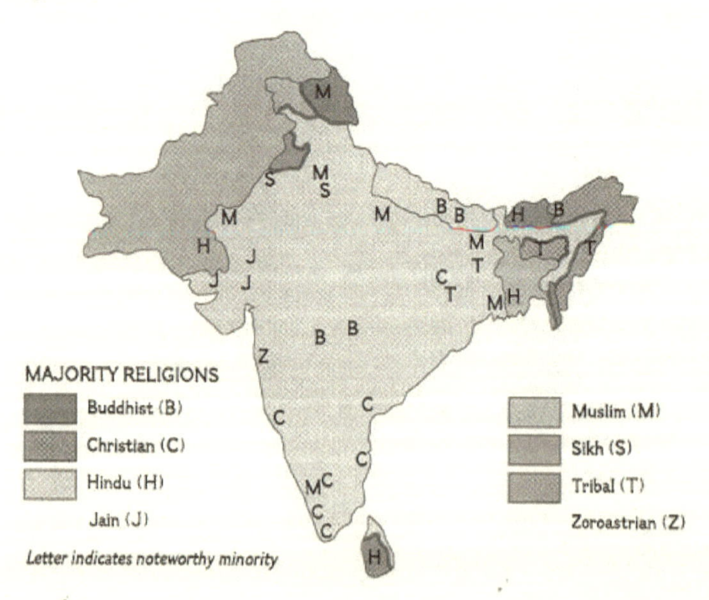

CHAPTER THREE

Rajiv Gandhi

Rajiv Gandhi Quotes

"Better a brain drain than a brain in the drain."

"Every person should take a lesson from history. We should understand that wherever there have been internal fights and conflicts in the country, the country has been weakened. Due to this, the danger from outside increases. The country has to pay a big price due to this type of weakness."

"Our task today is to bring India to the threshold of the twenty-first century, free of burden of poverty, legacy of our colonial past, and capable of meeting the rising aspirations of our people."

"When a big tree falls, the ground shakes."

"Education must be a great equalizer in our society. It must be the tool to level the differences that our various social systems have created over the past thousands of years."

"For some days, people thought that India was shaking. But there are always tremors when a great tree falls."

"Women are the social conscience of a country. They hold our societies together."

"India is an old country, but a young nation; and like the young everywhere we are impatient. I am young, and I too have a dream. I dream of an India strong, independent, and self-reliant and in the front rank of the nations of the world in the service of mankind."

"The terrorists are busy in and outside the country in such activities which are a danger to the unity and integrity of the country."

"The late Indira Gandhi always used to warn about the dangers that the country was facing. She used to keep saying that the country was going through a very dangerous time. This danger is now many times more than what it was at that time. We should all be cautious now."

"A responsive administration is tested most at the point of interface between the administration and the people."

"The world is changing much too fast for us to have a moribund system which is not flexible, which cannot evolve and develop with changes in our society, in our country, as they come about in the world."

"India missed the Industrial Revolution; it cannot afford to miss the Computer Revolution."

 "The thrust of our poverty alleviation programs is on the uplift of the farmers."

"Development is not about factories, dams, and roads. Development is about people."

India on the Map of the World

Administrative Map of India

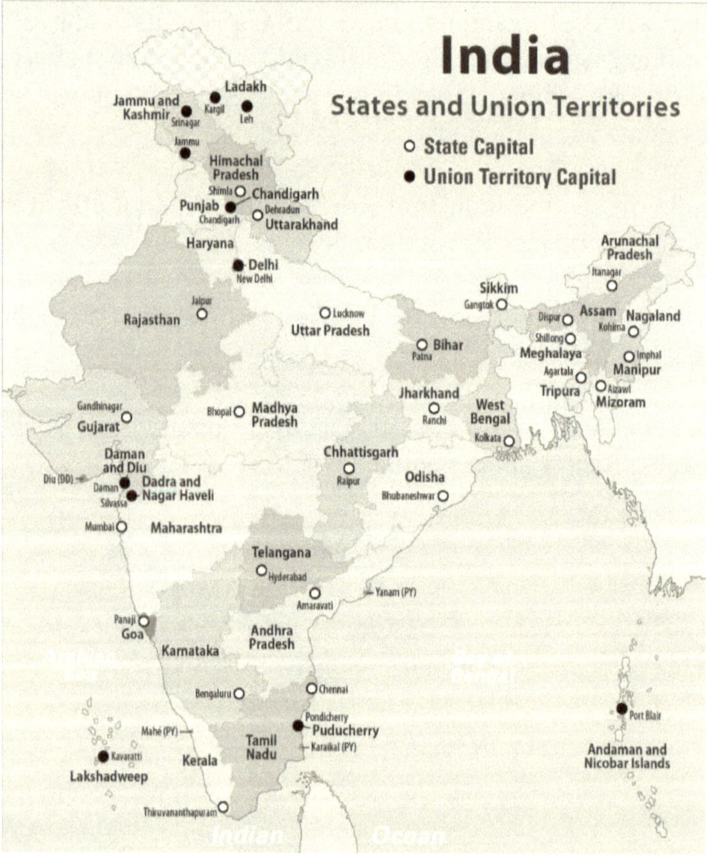

Born in Bombay, India on August 20, 1944, Rajiv Gandhi was the son of Indira Gandhi, the only female Prime Minister in India's history, thereby making him by default the grandson of the first Prime Minister of India Jawaharlal Nehru, who is equally secured in the annals of Indian history as one of the central figures in Indian politics before and after independence.

Rajiv Gandhi only got inducted into Indian politics by her mother after the death of his assertive younger brother Sanjay from an air crash on 23 June 1980 near Safdarjung Airport in New Delhi while Sanjay was performing an aerobatic maneuver.

Rajiv Gandhi went on to be elected in a by-election to the Lok Sabha (lower house of Parliament) and that same year became a member of the national executive of the Indian Youth Congress, the youth wing of the Indian National Congress party. From that first elected office, he went on to become the leading general secretary of India's Congress (I) Party (from 1981).

Unlike his younger brother Sanjay who was described as politically "ruthless" and "willful", especially in his prominent role as the prime mover in the state of emergency that her mother Indira Gandhi, then the prime minister of India, declared across the country, lasting from 1975-1977, following ongoing turbulences gripping the nation; Rajiv was regarded as a sympathetic and unimposing person who made it a point of consulting with other party members and who exercised a great deal of restraint that prevented him from making hasty decisions.

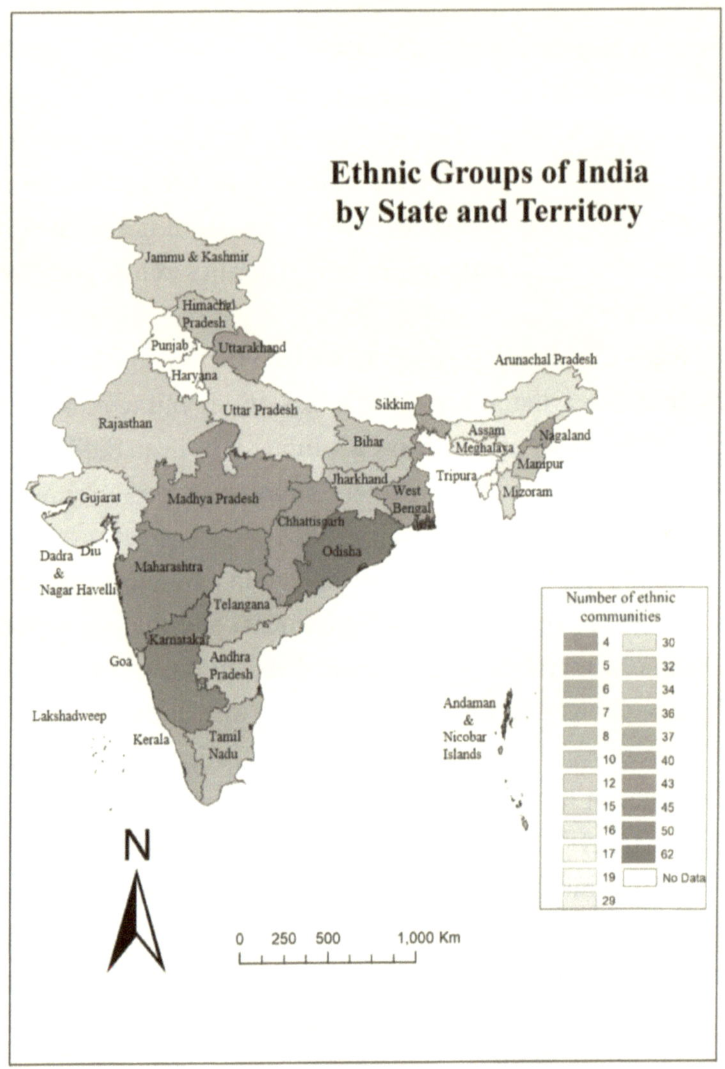

Following the death of his mother Indira Gandhi on Oct. 31, 1984, from gunshot wounds caused by the bullets of her Sikh bodyguards, Rajiv was sworn in as prime minister that same day and was elected leader of the Congress (I) Party a few days later. In December of that same year, he would lead the Congress (I) Party to a landslide victory in elections to the Lok Sabha in what could be considered an almost nationwide sympathy vote. This victory gave the Congress (I) Party it the largest majority to date in the Lok Sabha, the lower house of India's bicameral Parliament—411 seats out of 542.

Rajiv Gandhi and his administration set about reforming the government bureaucracy and liberalizing India's economy in a vigorous manner. However, he failed in his efforts to bring about peace, reconciliation, and quiet in the Punjab and Kashmir regions as the separatist movements there refused to budge. That and a series of financial scandals that rocked his government, compelled him to resign his post as prime minister in November 1989. However, he held onto his position as the leader of the Congress (I) Party.

On May 21, 1991, Gandhi was campaigning in Tamil Nadu for upcoming parliamentary elections when he and 16 others were killed by a bomb concealed in a basket of flowers carried by a woman associated with the Tamil Tigers, a militant Tamil organization based in northeastern Sri Lanka that had been waging a secessionist nationalist insurgency against the majority Sinhalese government of the country. The stated goal of the Tamil Tigers was to create an independent state for the Tamil people in the north and east of Sri Lanka that was to be called Tamil Eelam. Some Tamil Tigers thought Rajiv Gandhi was sympathetic to the Sinhalese majority in Sri Lanka because Sinhalese were Indo-Aryan speaking like most of the ethnic groups of

Northern India, unlike the Tamils that were Dravidian.

Map of Religious Minorities in India

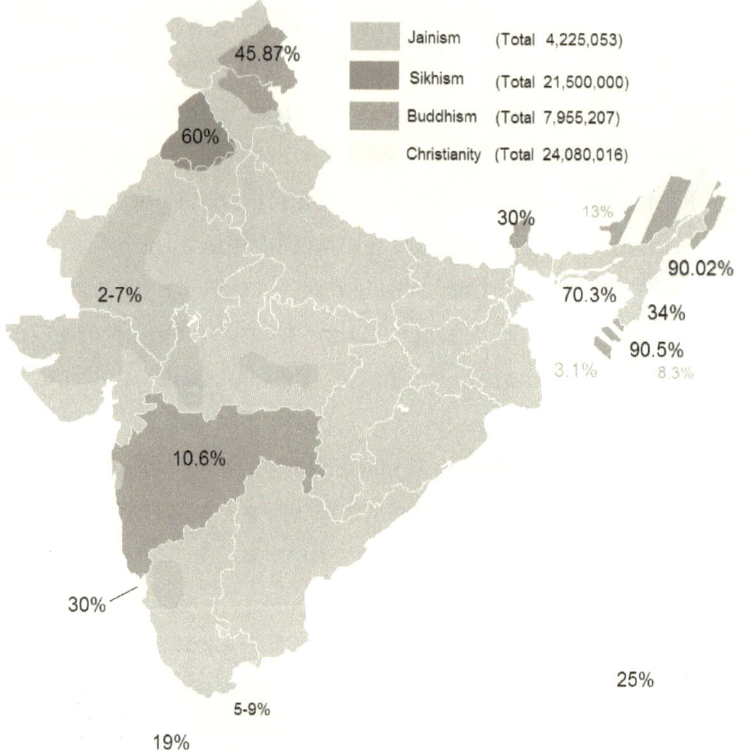

Rajiv Gandhi should have seen his death coming. It all started one year after the start of the Sri Lankan Civil War between the Liberation Tigers of Tamil Eelam (LTTE) and the Sri Lankan government, when Rajiv Gandhi sent the Indian Peace Keeping Force (IPKF) to Sri Lanka to protect civilians and to apprehend anyone carrying arms. The LTTE attacked the IPKF, compelling the IPKF to disarm them. This created a furor that forced Rajiv Gandhi to withdraw the IPKF from Sri Lanka in 1989. In fact, two years earlier, on 30 July 1987, an honor guard of Sinhalese background named Vijitha Rohana, hit him on his shoulder with his rifle, stating afterward that he wanted *"…to kill Rajiv Gandhi for the damage he had caused…"* to Sri Lanka. He was convinced that Rajiv Gandhi was supporting the Tamils, since the ethnic group was having portions of their homeland in Southern India and northern Sri Lanka. And this happened on July 30, 1987, a day after Rajiv Gandhi went to Sri Lanka and signed the Indo-Sri Lanka Accord with the Sri Lankan President J. R. Jayewardene.

The Indo-Sri Lanka Accord was expected to resolve the Sri Lankan Civil War by enabling the Thirteenth Amendment to the Constitution of Sri Lanka and the Provincial Councils Act of 1987, meaning that the government in the capital city of Colombo would devolve power to the provinces, withdraw Sri Lankan troops to their barracks in the north, and the Tamil rebels would disarm.

Of the hundreds of people arrested on grounds of involvement in the assassination of Rajiv Gandhi, 26 would be convicted by an Indian court in 1998 for involvement in the conspiracy. And as it turned out, the conspirators were Tamil militants from Sri Lanka and their allies in India, most of them ethnic Tamils themselves.

Linguistic Map of South Asia (Bangladesh, India, Pakistan)

War would flare up again between the Liberation Tigers of Tamil Eelam (LTTE) and the Sri Lankan government following Rajiv Gandhi's death, and it would be deadlier this time around so that at its peak in 2000, the Liberation Tigers of Tamil Eelam (LTTE) were in control of 76% of the landmass in the Northern and Eastern provinces of Sri Lanka where ethnic Tamils were the majority. In fact, the Tamil Tigers were in control of an area of 15, 000 km2 (5, 800 sq.

mi) at the start of the final round of the peace process in 2002. But then, the peace process would breakdown in 2006, the civil war would resume and the Liberation Tigers of Tamil Eelam (LTTE) would be crushed in a phase of the civil war that most pundits considered to be ruthless indeed, leaving the LTTE with no other option but to admit defeat on May 07, 2009. The death of the LTTE's leader Velupillai Prabhakaran two days after the surrender would all but bring the Sri Lankan civil war to a complete end, making it a conflict that resulted in the displacement of more than two million people and that caused more than one hundred thousand deaths (100, 000), one thousand two hundred (1, 200) of which were of the Indian Peace Keeping Force.

Today, a memorial called The Rajiv Gandhi Memorial sits at the site where he was assassinated at Sriperumbudur, India. Numerous works of art have been composed honoring the Indian prime minister.